CHANGING THE WINDOWS

Changing the windows

Jerome Mazzaro

OHIO UNIVERSITY PRESS
ATHENS, OHIO

For John and Eleanor Dimoff

ACKNOWLEDGMENTS

I would like to thank the John Simon Guggenheim Memorial Foundation for a fellowship, part of which was diverted to complete this manuscript. Many of the poems first appeared in *Accent, American Weave, Approach, The Colorado Quarterly, Epoch, Fresco, Fubbalo, The Galley Sail Review, The Mad River Review, The Massachusetts Review, The Minnesota Review, Noetics, Poetry Broadside, Quagga, Shenandoah, The Southern Poetry Review,* and *Triad.*

CONTENTS

CHANGING THE WINDOWS

1

Deserted by his flock, turned slightly yellow,
the sole survivor of some ancient ill,
the ivory shepherd boy catches my eye,
alone, unpacked, still resting near a window,
eyeing the crates stacked neatly near a wall
as if to pipe their final, soft goodbye.
Beyond him, past the glass, the lacy weave
of the huge elm tree forms its tracery
through which the white-slat houses of the block
appear like backgrounds to his steady gaze.
My stare goes out to some vague memory
strung like a wetwash in the inner eye
until a noise of traffic brings me back . . .
back to a morning I'd discovered him
while rummaging my grandmother's belongings,
and noticed in the eye two spotted tears
and on his back a ravaged, new-born lamb
and laid the tragedies to evil kings
who hired away an army of toy soldiers.
Now, years later, deserted by such realms,
I pack him out of habit when I leave
by choice or force one job for something better,
remapping what job-transferring assumes,
and having left all other boyhood games,
the armies having fallen to some grave,
marvel he still survives each hopeful future.

2

Only the last, quick, thorough scouring's left
before I load the crates into the car

3

and let go of the things we cannot take
for those to come like a considerate gift,
leaving the rooms we lived in all last year.
Looking about, I tackle this last work.
Strange, I had scoured them, too, when we arrived,
hoping by cleanser, ammonia, and soaps
to rid the former tenants from their walls.
Yet in the paint or a torn windowshade
they persisted, helping shape our hopes
which will assume their fulness someplace else.
I think of women, old friends once described,
who come to wash the dead with vinegar,
of the new tenants scrubbing us away,
and of the pictures hanging on our walls—
trees, people, landscapes, playful animals,
hearing in the small plaster holes we made
and where they used to hang, long hours of laughter,
hoping the sound survives their moving day.

3

So you can bid the animals goodbye,
we venture to the zoo to watch and sit
as we might do upon a sickroom visit
to someone close who is about to die.
But we're the ones who next week will be leaving.
The zebra with its thin stripes standing here,
after a spell indoors, will reappear
next year, never missing us or grieving.
So will the monkeys playing in their pen,
and the peacocks, those proud, deceptive things
who spread their god's-eyes to the sun mornings,
and, pacing the rocks, your favorite lion.
Propped on his bed, my father when he died
spoke of a magic voyage he would take

inside the cover of a Noah's Ark.
I remember this, standing at your side.
He showered me with all my favorite birds,
and made that going a processional
that transformed him into a special angel.
I missed and missed him deeply afterward.
It's we, the well, who always must be pampered.
And that you'll know this afternoon as happy
when these warm animals shrink to memory,
I offer cotton candy, popcorn, words.

4

Leaving this shady town for good,
car loaded down with moving crates,
I pass the willows and slow down,
my eyes still following the road
beyond a scattered file of graves,
and think of a bright afternoon
we picnicked in the willow groves.
Then you had asked, "What tree is that?"
"Willow," I said, and told a tale
of how the spirit of the tree
once changed into a shining girl,
married, and when the tree was cut,
at each ax blow showed agony.
A disbelief showed in your eye.

I told you, too, that Orpheus,
the greatest singer ever known,
when he went down to hell to bring
his love back carried such a bough,
and that some ancient shepherds sang
to flutes made out of willow trees.
An ivory shepherd, packed away,

reminds me of these days gone by—
uprootings, too, we've undergone,
and towns and friends we will incur,
as from one corner of my eye,
passing the county limits now,
I see a speed sign and glance down.
My speed's too slow. I press on faster.

A pirate-thinking child can do it,
escape the boundaries of a garden fence
for imaginary elm lands of the mind
and not lose sense.

He knows the crossbone grasses of the wind
and steers a squirrel nest with eyelids tight
that would leave weaker men, unused to it,
fisheyed with fright.

His object galleon, giant goldenrod,
floats spanishly across the morning breeze,
while like an unsuspected frigate, he
boom-booms the seas—

then boards and plunders her. The rustling tree,
rattling a warning of a void beyond,
conjures some boundary, but more flowers nod
and he sails on.

Always the threshold of a horse he stood,
his muzzle high, his stripes, his painted hoofs,
his manner, even the way he shied his food
through lonely passes where the clear blue cliffs
shone like the waiting outposts of each valley.
And yet they knew that he could never be,
for his close grooves even were only wood.
And through the distances of his quick stride
though children, breathing love, avoided proofs
and made him warm, thinking as well to free
his spirit, swearing, too, to hear him whinny,
always the threshold of a horse he stood.
And women riding with his reins in hand,
holding against the outbreak of his force,
gripped them the tighter as his move began
until their fear was what they rode upon
as they bent on in strange expectancy,
and yet they knew that he could never be.
The old men, too, spurring the creature on,
finding no praises that might charm his wood,
pressed their heels deeper in the sweating side
holding for their dear lives into a land
so lovely green that, though it stunned their reason,
always the threshold of a horse he stood.

i

Fighting those winds that ripped the canvas loose,
he went outside and tied the awning down
against new rains that rattled from the skies,
quelling the flap of what the winds had done
to weather newer storms just settling in.
Afterward, coming in skin-drenched, he'd wait,
prying the apron loose from his soaked shirt,
and watch as hard rain drenched the alley clean.
He sat as one with his guilt flooding out
until absorbed, caught in that rush, he'd feel
a sudden flash of anguish storm his face
that calm, resembled most a Dresden doll.
Once as a child he'd thought God's wrath the cause
like Noah's storm, and never shaking this,
he sought some past forgiveness as he moved,
praying a harm away from those he loved,
until a sky cleared and the sun's bright rays
showed once again a guilt had been absolved.

ii

Thus, though he'd sell red wine and bath-tub beer
and swap loud stories of his younger days,
the customers recall best in the store
items he wouldn't sell at any price—
a miniature of Antony whose face
peered through dry palm leaves, just above the reach,
beneath which a black rosary would stretch,
sent him from Italy and kept for mass
9   Sundays at Ste. Anne's brick, provincial church;

and statues of the Virgin, hard as glass
but made of china, settled in the hall
where neighbors, coming for their wine, would pass
and see them cap a simple pedestal—
those things he cherished with a private smile
fall mornings as he gazed at wife and son
busy at work before the store would open.
Later, he'd wait his trade like some clock's dial
ready with word or sale to make life happen.

iii

First off, the Sisters from the convent came
to buy what he'd reduced for a quick sale,
and while they picked his baskets for each item
he rambled on—as they searched in each stall—
about his homeland, how from one foothill
he could see Naples, and how houses lay
with small walled gardens off each major way;
and they, pretending not to hear, heard still,
to sense from it a Rome they'd never see.
His wife, as well, helping him straighten out,
would tell of Christ's Steps, how they both one day
saw white-coifed Sisters, rosaries held tight,
on their bare knees, pray up the steep stairway.
And always, finally when it came to pay,
there'd be small hassles and more prices cut,
not from their shrewdness but his own soft heart.
He'd say his Rocky would know Italy,
and draw in turn small prayers as they went out.

iv

And heir to merchant dreams that prospered then,
the boy took care to buy his father's lap

with bribes of nudging him from sleep each noon
and strutting like a braggard in his step.
He never felt the threatened razor strap
though once he stole a knife and brought it out
to two men fighting in the yard, his shout
of "Kill the bastard!" having caught them up
and held the tangled wrestlers and their fight
with laughter of another sort than fear.
The fear came later, crowding that long noon
at Mercy Hospital, when winter air
spun high in drifts against a frosted pane.
Inside, the worried grocer paced alone,
cut distant from the wife who sat nearby
hunched in a best cloth coat, afraid to cry,
as fears restepped the tense life of their son,
repeating, "Rocky must not die, not die."

v

Outside, converging, heightening the fears,
the faint, insistent, shrill and bronchial blurt
of darting children knifed into their ears.
Then grating sounds of a wheeled patient's cart
entered a silent hollow of the heart,
and he recalled his nephew's noisy wake,
the sirens when they fished him from the lake,
lodged lily-white and shapeless in a net.
Later, his sister said she used to shake
hearing the sound, until she grew so ill
she clutched at arms, yelling he wasn't dead,
so in the hospital where she is still
and outbursts strap her sometimes to her bed,
she mumbles, when she's lucid, how her head
is filled with blaring sirens, and her loss,
reflected like her sick-bed crucifix

in the globed crystal on her windowsill,
hangs her reversed like Peter on a cross.

vi

That night, still waiting, drowsed in his sickwatch,
he dreamed he was once more in Italy.
His child sick in bed, he went to fetch
fresh water from a well and stopped to see
the sky, spread strangely like a canopy,
a smell of flowers, faint, medicinal,
stale as that wafted through a hospital.
There snow-capped mountains lined before his eye—
each point exact to what he could recall.
Within the hush of that hypnotic scene,
he paused to make an urgent, new request
to speed a safe recovery for his son.
Things moved then of themselves in more unrest
that dazzled him as streets soon shifted past,
and suddenly as a new silence spread,
a shooting star and Antony appeared
and hung above a nearest mountain crest.
They argued long, intensely overhead.

vii

This Antony would plead to save the son
against a steady, unrelenting fall
of "Never. No, no. It cannot be done.
The boy must die," until these words were all.
Frightened, the figure let his buckets spill,
turning to note hushed figures up ahead.
Home, he found Rocco lifeless, sprawled in bea,
his sister loudly screaming by a wall
of some strange curse they'd both inherited.

The days confirmed the dream despite his prayer.
A rosary was buried with the boy,
while he—the statues and the miniature
removed—grew angry as a child with toy.
He slipped them in a paper sack one day,
and muttering "They're useless as bad checks,"
he shut the store against his friends' respects,
and hiked across the fields of fallen snow
past the town trash heap to old railroad tracks.

viii

Knowing that though they learned to value sales
his dream would not be filled by any son,
that like his sister in her lucid spells
he was beset by forms who would not own
his prayers in a strange pact he sensed was broken,
and which no future son could reunite,
nor find the pieces having come too late,
he asked that they be free of what he'd done.
Calmly accepting then this first defeat,
he struck reprisal in a lightning blow,
breaking the Virgin's heads against the ties,
and watched as splinters sank into the snow.
He shattered Antony across their loss,
vowing a life-long enmity on those
lies of beneficence and former powers
he'd paid his homage to in other years.
Then confident of nothing more to lose,
He searched the sunlight's cold for their shrill tears.

"It is in loving the Cross that one finds one's heart, for
divine love cannot live without suffering."

Marie-Bernard Soubirous

i

His too-large skull draws in to form the cheeks,
bone-grey and crackling, raging at the wall
whose stained-glass windows float a speckled pall
on Francis, white, affected underneath.
His tortured stare ignores what that saint seeks
in catechumens' learned and practiced rote—
the statuary calm of marble birds.
Quiescence is the food those tongues bequeath.
His parching lips suspend a different note
to frighten boys a wayward wandering
and give full conscience to the practiced words
whose chant let run like songs might merely skim
the causes for this endless suffering,
bending at will by turns from seeing Him.

ii

Sister Blondina skirts a classroom floor,
beating a catechism with her rule.
Small-voiced, she calmly tells us not to fool
Omniscience, but take our textbooks home—
coughing an interim of lungs' uproar—
and pray for love of awkward, raging forms
whose deaths redeem mankind his fitful soul.
Her phrases drive our minds, too used to roam
for warmth and shelter from her coughing storms,

like birds about Saint Francis, carolling
that sterner peace she offers as our goal.
White like his birds, one fall she ventured south
and did not venture back the coming spring.
We students dim the prayers of her mouth.

iii

Christ, make me good like Francis standing here,
and smiling, simple-minded, lacking stress,
rich in the joys of statued saintliness
and blandness, telling easy ways of life
which fatted till a reformation fear
ate capon out of its rich progeny
and glutted into white and peaceful spires.
Your pitted eyes emit a deeper knife
to probe my squirming flesh its constancy.
I terrify the wonder and Your strain,
can't emulate the form; my body tires,
hates bones, deformity, Your bloody palm,
the real and practiced art of looking pain,
and wishes taste, good manners, gloried calm.

iv

Father Maguire, girt in a cleric's gown,
walks down the aisle of a Monday church
to chat away all fear and vainly search
our chants for simple dread of sin's abyss.
Sometimes a gentle, everseeing clown,
he teases Sisters, shows us tricks, will say,
"Sister Bambina," add a private joke.
Father, the years have rent a precipice
between us. Southering that later day,
you winged His face, spewing your blood for spit

and shook me to the beauty of His look.
Gongs ring us back. Your face, outrageous, beams,
downing the milquetoast trappings in that fit,
pulling the walls about me with your screams.

The buildings of this town have been their pride—
worn, nineteenth century symbols of restraint;
yet those who learn to see beneath the paint
might notice here a rot that pigments hide
and judge streets by the sounds of settling tile,
the groans of plaster, tossings of a bed,
the loose slate softly shifting overhead,
monsignor's black and sticky, spidery smile.

Watchful, he's seen the inroad the rot makes,
how white paint near the ground is first to go.
The pinewood then, beneath the front bay window,
nibbled by age peels suddenly and slakes.
He's made his stands against this laxity,
especially in the poorer parts of town
where he's told people not to get rundown.
Yet struggles with the poor have made him weary.

He's weary, too, of youngsters taking cars
into the country for strange, nightly spins
far from their parents' homes where nothing happens
so that their headlights haunt the hills like stars,
for in these headlights he sees that night's aim,
star-stuck, enticing, nudging near to rest
warm hair against some arm or gym-built chest.
Pregnancy's become a major problem.

And at the college, nestled on one hill,
he's sensed professors at their weekly tea
paint and repaint a moral bankruptcy
so often that their motives seem quite real,
and wondered in their little injuries

if after balancing their teas and biscuit,
there's no long struggle with an inner rot,
but presses someone's arm and turns away.

The merchants, too, inside the bank's new apse,
having kept unions and high wages out,
applaud his earnest, solitary effort
to keep land values from a feared collapse,
and like quick flies above a crystal stream,
when he gets down to facts and figures, slip,
lauding the honest, steady stewardship,
beyond what webs he's slyly cast for them.

Still every autumn he insures the church
and tells his parish of the year's repairs,
warning the niggardly parishioners
the pocketbook, not heart, 's the place to search,
and noticing their struggling interest drop
adjusts his mike so everyone can hear
and shouts how only the male wolf spider
and man are known to force their love to rape.

Because she willed it, flowers flowed the brooks
those seasons of the year when water stirred,
and real as butterflies or stones they'd shine,
white-petalled in the winter's snowy discard.
She plucked them to her mind, building her world:
the gardens, porpoise, and the velvet curtains,
and names so rich in their foreign cadences
that each one moved like valleys into blossom.
Her neighbors, though, she never moved: up, down,
or sideways. They stood firm as the mountains
only larger on the window edge and blared,
jostling her fingers always from the petals,
to where winds touched on her too common looks
and reeled a street where fishermen would shout
or those grim faces answer through a transom.
Even her curtains could not keep them out.

Large waterlilies burst the pond,
and, daughter, you go out to them—
separate as buttons on your dress
and spotted with the morning dews—
playing a silly little game
that strands me here holding your hand.
I wait. The glitter of your eyes
over the shallow waters' flow
calls back to this safe, balding father
who diets yearly to keep slender,
old days he'd sooner trade for you,
who, vanished into some wide blur
of grassy, shade-drenched trails ahead,
belie those foolish fantasies.
Then obediently you return
to fetch me to this sight, and while
you stand here as a knowing guide
who'd lead me down a tricky road
explaining each minute pitfall,
a whiteness strikes, taking us in.

Already they bear the body to the church,
altar societies, monks, priests,
and then the corpse, followed by
an empty hearse and screaming women,
ending with his friends.

Already, too, they're talking of the daughter
who couldn't leave her work to visit him,
and while they set him in his grave,
she joins the other legends of the town—
The woman who was pitchforked and then burned.
To this day no one knows for sure by whom,
though there are rumors.
And the other who was knifed and stuffed
into a grotto by a looney
everyone thought harmless until then.
And the woman who was chased off her own
property with a shotgun
by her brother
and died of outrage shortly afterward.
And finally the girl who went beserk
waiting for someone to marry her
and turned into a prostitute,
sometimes waking the whole town up
with her wild, enticing rages.

She will be saved as they are saved
for the warm winter fires
when conversations lag.
Someone will say, Do you know what happened to . . . ,
and then it will all come out,
year after year, generation after generation,
21   after even the father has been forgotten.

Nine windmills thresh the furrows of the sun.
It is dusk, their shadows curve
long muscled arms against a ripened field,
threshing the disappearing grain.
Such are the giants now, and one
astride his chair, reading his newspaper,
sits reminded of the fierce storms
tumbling across the mountaintops
when there were foolish hopes and heroes
brawling like drunkards over ale,
imagining in those scraps
ghosts trammelling the dusk, piercing time,
and clashing blades, grinding
like John Deere reapers out across the hall.
And fingering a belly's flab,
the wheatfields having disappeared,
he goes indoors to draw
his covers in a winter snowstorm
white and dreamily about his flesh.

Sweet williams gutter pink
along the walk, fisting the fallen snow,
    and seeing them, how can one think—
bundled in parka or in mackinaw,
    his tightened face nipped pink as flowers—
        to turn them back to summers?

Riding this air, the kids
bulk parkas sledding swiftly down the dunes,
    leading their summers into skids.
And warmly, without pity, summer's gone
    like runners through a flowergarden
        leaving the stalks to harden.

In Milford's hardened walls,
crew-out and cassocked, they abandon time,
    the winter winds caught dipping squalls
across the cloisters like a pendulum,
    the vespers and the matins marking
        quick seasons with their passing.

The lovers out of season,
hands caught in warmer hands, as tightly fist:
    the winter flowerings their reason,
their love converging flurries in their midsts.
    Caught up like bits of colored paper,
        the bright sweet williams flutter.

You were the king—at least you claimed to be—
of shoving landslides and a fractured knee,
and we all bowed to you, taking your side
in this and that. We even helped you hide
when William came and told him you were dead
or gone. I don't remember which we said,
but he believed our tale and claimed your crown
and golden birds for having knocked you down.
You went away one winter. Exile, I think.
It's so confusing now. It was the brink
of Christmas and the snow (The telegram
came later, that I'm sure.) had covered tram
and trolley tracks. It was in all the books—
killed by a sniper near the river Luxe.
And all of Hastings Street sent masses out,
even gulled William, who began the rout.

Death was a trick I taught him as a pup
like fetching till he mastered both to race
my ordered stick back clamped between his jaws,
ignoring once too soon the whir of trucks
whose chirring crushed whole worlds of growing up
and set him broken in a makeshift box.
Across blind roadways he comes running yet,
small-terriered, black-footed, slow in death.

The pages of her book spread like a snow
on the familiar mountains.
In their print she sees the tracks of a hare
and takes off following, up into the peaks.
She's always breathless from the climb,
sensing her cheeks take color from the air
so that's she's beautiful, her dark warm hair
brilliant in the winter skies.
One marvels at her perseverance, at her calm.
She merely answers it's her home;
from the height she's able to see her parents' chimney,
small and singular in the valley
as she's done on all her other climbs.
Her mother's at the door waving. It's still light;
her father's with the animals.
Often she looks up from the book and waves to them,
but the hare keeps on, and she, after it.

That threaded brilliance, Hannibal in silk
gaping the elephants and fat as grouse,
his faded flesh the color of whole milk
against an armor's faded, silvery blues,
preserves the man as he was pictured once:
He stands among six well-groomed elephants,
plotting a final march on frightened Rome,
perfect except for stains left by the years,
which even careful cleanings cannot dim,
weaving a second tale upon his first.
One stain, the faded yellow of beef broth,
suspends his middle. I watch the tapestry,
my mother reading Invernizio
aloud, and think the stain some blood, for she
has told me blood stains fade a yellow.
Perhaps some prince was knifed against the cloth
as in her books? Savonarola waged
his war with Rome and pillaged Florence both
its art and men after the weaver staged
this scene; his heresy might cause such stains.
Or old Lorenzo, vomiting his pains,
dying, refusing finally to give in
to that disloyal monk he'd valued once,
deprived at last of his last absolution,
resting where his sleep's sweeter than a stone's.
Her voice absorbs. Caught in its dulling rounds
of family feuds and deadly treacheries,
I fight my boyish mind for English sounds,
staring beyond our arbor at the trees
that weave the borders of her Roman world
until I'm drowsed like Florence going mad,
or Hannibal among his milling herd,

27

waging a future, harmless, reckless raid
like Charles against a Vatican Swiss Guard,
staining my war with drops of lemonade.

B = 47 Athletic Field Rd., Waltham, Mass. 02154

C = 1312 27th Street, Zion, Illinois 60099

D = P. O. Box 10007, Denver, Colorado 80210

E = Richard Abel & Co. (England) Ltd., 6A Mill Trade Estate, Acton Lane, London N.W. 10, England

F = Richard Abel & Co., AG, Fischerweg 9, 3002 Berne, Switzerland

H = P. O. Box 241, Marion, Ohio 43302

J = P. O. Box 15469, Atlanta, Georgia 30333

K = Richard Abel & Co., Pty., Ltd. 1/33 Warraba Road, Narrabeen North, N.S.W. 2101 Australia

L = 1506 Gardena St., Glendale, California 91204

N = 1001 Fries Mill Rd., Blackwood, New Jersey 08012

P = P. O. Box 4245, Portland, Oregon 97208

S = Industrial Center Bldg., Gate 5 Road, Marinship, Sausalito, California 94965

T = Richard Abel & Co. (Canada) Ltd., 128 Industrial Rd., Richmond Hill, Ontario, Canada

X = 3434 Dalworth St., Arlington, Texas 76010

OHIO UNIVERSITY PRESS

CHANGING THE WINDOWS.

MAZZARO, JEROME.
ATHENS, OHIO, UNIVERSITY PRESS 1966

64 P. 23 CM.

BOOK NO.

4|75

40

The winter smells lodge in our frontroom wall
like troublesome boarders who've refused to quit,
giving the room a sense of the eternal
of family histories settling there with soot.

And there my old maiden aunt sits waiting death,
repulsive in her age, scratching her scalp
as I sit watching, hating every breath
with each blown fart or belch or need for help.

To get her out last spring we planted turnips
but had to watch her mornings when she'd water
to keep her from those garrulous, humped gossips
who'd pry our secrets from her mindless chatter.

Once she refused the banker's last proposal,
sitting there teasing like a piquant goose—
a girl of twenty-five, her rich mantilla
shading that ripeness she could not let loose.

And now she falls on us like earth's upheaval.
We're always working to offset her loss,
spending our nights at home at her disposal.
Had she just taken him, she'd been his cross.

Only the church's patrons list still courts her.
That greedy, shrivelled-up, hell-spouting ass
who gave me first communion, he supports her.
He stuffs her full of Christ and heaven's grace.

When I am forced by circumstance and heat
to take the winter windows off the house
spotted like bass who will be stripped of lice,
I think of that old woman down the street
who got by the Depression renting rooms
to seven lonely bachelors in a row,
the last of whom fell from an open window
changing the screens one sunny afternoon.
Called Mother Witch by city columnists
who wrote how all the seven perished strangely,
each with an ample, paid-up policy
made out to her, she didn't snare one jurist
in all the headline months her trials ran—
though winter changed to summer as it must.
She sat reading a favorite *Evening Post*
as if no court could judge her for her sin.
Thinking, too, of her full-grown idiot son
who scavenged in our ashcans after that
feeding himself with cast-off bits of fat
until a court ruled he'd too lost his reason,
somehow I think of husbanded black widows
and savage birds who sometimes eat their young,
and wonder at the web this world becomes,
then scuttle off to unhinge all the windows.

All morning she sits kneading bread,
reminded by the flour of snow,
her thoughts a frail, snowlost swallow
in winter. Dinner must be laid.
So she brands thought some foolishness,
dispensing plates like charity
among members of her family.
Still it brings back those hanukahs,
beautiful, half-mysterious,
when snow piled nightly in huge drifts
and relatives came bringing gifts.
She always wore a brightest dress.
The dress she wears wanes as a moon
as she shapes bread for the oven
and sits to wait four hungry children,
beggars or birds, who'll fly home soon.

From those stiff gathers, formal as the pose
which brings me here this noon,
the trees go dun,
the motley leaves about us settle gauze,
and posters' tattered, pasteboard almond trees,
grown flakes by time, defect
on our too perfect
bearings, stiffened to the paper's flurries.

A furled umbrella slants against your dress,
stiff as a new-bloomed rose,
while my look goes
meandering across the public grass
to where two playing children spin to stone
so that their gaudy blur
turns an old banner,
their forms like waves recede into our own.

I think of our twin girlhoods come to stone,
and of your husband, sprawled
dead in that field,
scattered among the wreckage of a train
while this safe duck-pond gathered and a duck,
oily and dun, swam near,
throating to bear
that martial stiffness which his body struck.

And your own stiffness like a public mask
against the warmth we'd chance
as children once,
then always to be brought later to task
like these ducks out of water, seeking grace.

Father would call us down,
and with his frown
insist we sit like stumps on that stilled terrace.

Francis's almond trees, once tapped of floods,
went bitter into sweet,
the conduit
a balance to their moderation's needs.
What balance to these old civilities?
Lacking all signs of flow,
we wrap a snow,
mind-driven to our wills' self-postured ease.

What is the act to stir us into strife?
Settled, we seem to wait,
to ruminate
like hollow waxworks on the edge of life,
where watching we both stiffen to the past
as if its injuries
charged these dull skies
and shaped the worlds about us to their test.

I start to say, "He chose that way to die,
fighting a fascist Spain . . . "
as if some bargain
he'd made with life loving could not deny,
as my nun's habit points my own ideal,
or your each finished poem.
"Dad wants you home
to spend some time with him until you're well."

"He was quite gentle," you begin to say,
and seem a continent,
long worlds distant.
"He used to join the children in their play."

Idealism has its price. We both know that,
having in ways become
as well its victim.
Alternatives are pointless as regret.

"Perhaps if I had had a child, why then
his duty might be flesh.
I wish, I wish . . . "
It was impossible you know again,
and guilt like blood runs quickly to your face.
I want to tell you, Pray.
The "sister's way,"
I think, easy, absurd, and now as pointless.

"Look near your shoulder, starlings shake the air."
And shocked by their display,
a sudden sway,
the woven leaves about us start to tear
as the whole park goes suddenly piecemeal.
We both get up to go.
Today, tomorrow,
light will break each rigid background sentinel.

i

Beyond your face snow blizzards in the walk
we rode, two children on a rusty sled,
and bends beside the tree whose limbs held talk,
our secrets, and whose summer apples fed
our tummy aches until a cousin carved
his name too deep inside the bark and starved
both fruit and our green years. The tree,
turned black, bends yearly since, while we
from different paths return each Christmas day
to whet our lives against its treachery,
renewing guilt like friends in its dark sway.

ii

You come fat-jowled, a nun with a valise,
to spend an hour and I from my new book
to note the difference that the years increase.
How hard for us to share a common look!
You sit, your features countenanced by sound,
by matins and the schoolbells breaking ground
at Ste. Anne's small provincial, brick-walled school;
or watching children flock your office stool
to learn of God and man, and share your laughs
at Father's jokes, sprouting the Order's rule
like miracles of flowers from dried staffs.

iii

I sit, your twin, my features fixed by words,
by all the vast descriptions of my books,

the summer apple dreams whose mockingbirds
brim apple blossoms, and the treeside brooks
unable now to warm the whirling snow,
for love drove white inside its gnarling glow
and passing years pressed people giving pain
to energies for re-creation's strain,
as in the summers all the leaves would once
break down by actions reason can't explain
sun's force to fulness, dreams to common sense.

iv

And in these flurries, even snowbanks spill
the dark, obtrusive towers shadows reign,
imaginary monarchs, will on will,
planning our Tudored girlish lives to gain
those arts that shinny up a tree, and go
fastest and longest in the piling snow.
Then that communion day, and someone's dare
shinnied us up into the leafy air
and scraped our dresses, turning Father's voice
into the violent flow of his despair
and ended all these willful worlds by choice.

v

Our Father, that vast shadow on the tree,
bends massive, dark, conservative, and dim,
to compromise rule after rule that we
might toe a mental line described by him
and kept by Mother, who with her deep glance
tatted and knitted their arranged romance.
Not being boys, he frowned our tomboy ways,
telling us how from our maturing thighs
would come his stock, like a great corded fruit

to fill the harvest of his winter days
with apple-cheeking grandsons and repute.

vi

Then in that fateful spring, our cousin came
in his Stuts Bearcat and bright uniform
straight from Montmartre's still-scandalizing fame
bringing our childhood to end while the warm,
still budding blossoms of the apple tree
fell sweet beneath our bursting weights and he,
like history's naif swain, cut in the bark
our two initials as a second ark
to float the waves of love that flooded there
across the meetingplaces after dark
that were secure from Mother's cinctured stare.

vii

All spring we floated on that crested dream
until one morning from the Hartford train
a screw-faced woman waded through the steam,
our cousin's wife, to challenge his disdain
and settle down with him beyond the run
whose white-slat houses festered in our sun.
And Father sighed, glad to hush up the troth,
sternly philosophizing to us both
how this was best, and love began to close
as blossoms in an early summer's growth
to hide the sprouting fruit a stigma grows.

viii

Now in the silence, drifting snowbanks still
the meetingplace beside that summer path

the night I took a midwife's bloody pill
and saved our honors from the stormy wrath
of Father's looks, fearing this righteousness
more than the deathly pallor of my face,
until our worried parents sensing why
called private doctors, thinking I might die,
and you made promises to God for health,
setting your fervent cap in that dull lie
that made me heiress to their sterile wealth.

ix

Firm in that single road, you prospered there,
content, forgiving, and a penitent,
within the House's brickish Oxford air,
learning by rules to be more diligent,
to lose yourself in robes as in the laugh
you quelled across your convent photograph.
I wrote you then, as I envisioned you,
a white-robed stork among the goose-girl's blue,
and tried the city whose fruit-carted lane
caught up the dying apple tree, these two,
and gave me room to seed my dreams again.

x

Tomorrow you will come and we shall talk,
exchanging gifts beside this Christmas tree,
and tour this house, the snow-swept garden walk.
Sometimes I tell you, too, the ecstasy
that filled my life the brief months afterward
before I came back saddened to this yard
deadened by Mother's stare, to Father's side.
I needed warmth, as ouzels need their hide,
to teach me warmth. I could not love your Stream,

that effluence of air where you abide;
I needed ghosts and pain to fill my dream.

xi

And they who set us on these separate roads
died shortly afterward; he from his wife,
and they, our parents, from their martyr loads,
while we reached out for roots to build a life.
Tonight the snow has made me think of them,
these four, whose love exposed my gift of whim
and sent your love, expansive as your mind,
too soon to bear the duties of your kind.
Our parents would be proud of your small fame.
The tree, our childless selves, caught in the wind,
comes crackling down the yard that was their name.

Such was the season when the fear began:
the windless wheatfields stretching out like blight,
the neighbors moving cattle to the sun,
the tongue still thickening inside the throat,
and in the morning, carts going into town,
their lowing cows brindling the morning sky,
their axles winding into the horizon
like lean pigs muzzling to a broken sty.
Roadside a boy sits watching, fearful, his eye
cast where the road dips westward out of sight,
out of the long suns which had scorched lands dry
into the yearnings that had been his night.
His shirt flaps out into the arid breeze
the carts throw up; his eyes begin to rise
and fingers stroke the dog whose button eyes
crack like the sun-dried farmlands of his gaze.
Searching the lands for any signs of growth,
the blue shirt sleeve still warding off the sun,
as silently the farmer wipes his mouth
and lets his muscles slacken from their strain.
Inside the house, the woman dishes oats,
her face grown bleaker in this rainless weather,
eyes turning in where pity has run out
and girlish hopes like roadsides come together.
And even in the distance, past full trees
the rises glower like bleached skulls of cows
and gypsy wagons full of pleasantries
creak through the noontime to appointed rounds.
Someday when clouds come too, someday not yet,
the boy knows sure he'll lead a cow to pasture
and understand the fear and not forget—
40   someday when rainclouds come and shape the future.

One follows each detail,
rare woods and sober-colored lacquer, scrolls,
each tree, stone, spreading pond ripple,
learning house and garden
designed as one are one from each new view,
house to garden to house.

Tea masters come to mind,
arrangements of their famous abstract gardens
where one saw only stones and plants,
water become white sand;
rock, sandfall, vegetation turned to one,
life as some painter paints.

Such gardens, once designed
for beauty's contemplation, thought's mere use,
approached by the most narrow paths
of time-eroded stone,
were thus set off from everbrowning swaths
of mountainside and town.

Green as a sea monster's
strange, soft skin the lawn here slithers awake,
azalea, jasmine on its neck,
smooth rocks from riverbanks,
bushes rising on its outmost haunches,
fading pines and maples;

across the stone doorway
to ward off evil spirits a small screen
so they who come here, pondering
the mind's immense blue depths

from which those monsters fiercer than the lawn
emerge, may feel no fright.

To such a place when winds
rattle the brown leaves loose from the gold trees
and air and stem no longer hold,
like jars the fingers fold,
tenderly as the changing mountainsides,
to house the falling leaves.

He had been prepared for death,
but as in the books:
neighbors taking down his final breath,
the women weeping,
but Death suddenly tripped him.
Now his sisters say a eulogy
as if about a stranger
and in the spring a niece
makes a trail between the gravestones and crosses;
and the bees who know no sadness
come flying because of the flowers.

Fruit rebels into blossom.
The bees,
exactly as the ones last year,
compose its honey.
I'm tired of this merry-go-round.
I want to find a country
where everything is in reverse:
where clocks crawl backwards,
and the days and years turn backwards,
and the past is there ahead
like a mud-caked girl on a corner
feeding squirrels—
always on a brink of womanhood.

i

As those faint shadows that once tumbled down
from the ribbed ceilings of Ste. Anne's brick church,
the shadows of these metal flutings lurch
in the plane's creases to a steady fall
of silence, deadening as a nun's dark gown.
And coifed above the motors' anchorings
outside, more darkness tumbles to the plane
so what one thinks about in the hummed lull,
wrapped in the shiney metal scaffoldings,
is you telling us green communicants
how like good trees good fruit should be our sign,
adding a story to remove all doubt
how Gertrude holding love to sin's advance,
like Cyril at Jerusalem's main gate,
sensed cleansing flames burning her devils out.

ii

Last leave when I was home a silence spread
to the drab, cindered churchyard where we ran
as boys, and pausing at the churchdoor then,
I saw new boys marshalling a game of war
where nothing but a schoolbell woke their dead,
and thought how sons of immigrants we took
those simple lessons pounded by your rule,
wide-eyed as saints above the center altar,
drinking our knowledge deeply from each book
to reach that point where we reversed their trade.
Inside, drawn to the crucifix's pull
and pain-etched ugliness, that once struck fear,

I sought your words, burst like a mustard seed—
"Art will show beauty where none was before."—
and feeling chilled, left by a nearest door.

iii

This afternoon I tried to stall that fear
that warned me we'd be taking off tonight
by writing, then deciding not to write
and playing cards instead, sipping straight gin.
You came back then, a bolt shot from nowhere.
But write what? bombing takes one's faith away
when mission after mission towns beneath
flicker and fire against a grey pre-dawn
like candles at the altar where you pray?
or that your talks on love and charity
have gone the same way as your talks on faith?
that destructive power, night after night,
becomes addictive so one must destroy?
that thought merely makes us joke about it?
I wrote of weather and was too polite.

iv

Sister, what we sense here is life not art
widening and widening in the winter snow
where soon a burst of bomb and home will glow
like some abstract-impressionistic blur—
bits of your stained-glass windows!—and my heart,
refusing to accept the pure design,
sinks deeper in despair where years from now
I'll search the shadows for my being here,
or worse, forget the injuries I'd done,
telling myself that this like sickly skin
must be removed to let a healthy grow,

that separate acts like colors stay entire—
fragments, not fusions leaded!—and just then,
our target looms into its zero hour.
We roll, and all turns flak and spark and fire.

Put up no monument, but let the winds
in grasses sound his innocence, and place
hydrangea in clusters on his grave.
He was your brother. He was brave.
Your kinship binds you to a single face.
He needs no other tending but the winds.

He rode the waves at Guam, first casualty
of that beachhead, his bashed face in the sand.
At home he took you to the picture shows
or taught you baseball. His furloughs
like his forearms took your wildness in hand
to teach you patience, hugged against his clothes.
You never understood his casualty.

Hearing, you shied our arms for your locked room
and slid his photograph inside a drawer,
then left his uncompleted letter mussed
to hug your desk, defiant as the dust;
and would not go to movies about war,
becoming silent as his empty room.

The church was silence, belled against his bier.
Old buddies preached a homily of praise
beside a flag-draped coffin yards from you
while you roved distant in the closest pew.
Their speeches could not penetrate your haze
nor comments stir you from your childish view
that would not know the bones inside the bier.

Then like an inning's change, you grew to love
that stringy girl who floated through your walls.

48

Walking with you to school, she held your side,
teasing that wildness you strove to hide
with gestures of her love. We watched from halls
her awkward forms, your growing ease of love.

Coldly you struck All Souls' Day and his grave
to chance a look; standing a moment hushed,
you found the painted cross without a mar,
wanting no elegance, and said your prayer.
Your private monument to him is crushed?
Erect no other. He is no god of war.
His playfields are the oceans of the grave.

He AWOLed second night in camp,
that hellekin whose shyness poised
in silver cords or so we noised
through Sicilies of rant and ramp.
Against the flight, the startled cry
of hoot-owls flapping at the pitch,
two rabbits rustling from a ditch,
a pale moon silvering the sky.
Later we found him near a swamp,
dishevelled, gibbering of a bitch,
a Judy of a roadside tramp
who came to him at finger's twitch.
He knew her twice in that warm place,
the marsh gas burning its green glow—
both as a lover whose smooth flow
pressed sparks into her rutted face.
Now in our world, his fingers trace
marks of the frantic world gone loon,
etching into each packingcase
scars of the night's still paling moon.

Those greenish lines that will not touch the ground
are trees; those box-like sorts of ovals, heads;
and yellow spilling in one corner sets
the scene for daylight and a grey-blotched hound.
He doesn't notice yet the plashing reds
which line the paintbox. Sometimes he forgets
and paints them later as bright flowerbeds.
Yet there's a realness to the simple world
he paints; disjunctive strokes that seem to lead
even an eyeless father into seeing
the strange dimensions which a sight has jarred:
a dog, too out-of-size even for a weed;
and weeds so tall they dwarf a human being
in giant stalks that will not grow to seed.
Still these small figures touch a deeper sense
than stalks or large immensities of sky,
their faces turned defiantly toward green.
He finishes. The flashes of his fingers clench
a last droll stroke; then placing of an eye,
and he leans back, withdrawing in the scene,
blood-red against a father's blood red thigh.

1

Along the rugged coast a snowy froth
    edges the sea to sea,
and on the hills a duplicating mist
    whitecaps the ruins of ancient shores
      outlined against the skies.

Thinking such things exempla of a world
    returning to the eye
a natural optic law, the Greeks set down
    and founded in Syracuse stones
      and families still intact

to mark the birthplace of a patroness
    of sight, who seeing saw
beyond their closed and simple natural laws
    of self-reflection to a sight
      more lifting than herself.

No wonder when Columbus saw these hills
    cutting the ocean's calm,
he named them thus: with their abundant snakes
    and deadly spiders making law,
      one hardly thinks on life.

2

Because the journey has attained success,
    I know you will be pleased:
The harbors here are wide and in excess,
    their great varieties of plants unshed,
      studded with winter ants.

And mountains here abound with gold and ores;
    and natives so like ants
move through the leaves, carrying sharpened spears,
   but always take to flight like birds
    whenever we make night.

Regards their humor, they have greater love
    for others than themselves,
and willingly give valuables for trash
   and speak one language and seem ripe
    for gleanings of our Lord.

How right and wonderful that Ferdinand
    should snare the ghostly gems
of their conversions for his noble land.
   Let all of Christendom rejoice
    and welcome this new wealth.

3

Co-co-co-clicking in the old man's pouch,
    the tide and tide of bones
and frenzy rising upward from the night
   cancel the sighs his stomping drones,
    releasing all to night.

Go catch the black tarantula in the hand,
    and if he doesn't bite
or kill you like an unsuspecting ant,
   you'll have the magic gift of sight
    to guide your guiding hand.

Or take the scorpion in between the toes
    and see what he will do.
If either bites, then dance the poison through

until it sweats from you in streams
and leave such special dreams.

Paying the *houngnan* with his only gold,
the young man sets for home:
across the hilltops the first legs of dawn
which he would take into his hold;
at foot, the scorpion.

4

Only the natives live for any time
in this pestiferous place
where one is always near the famed Soufriere
whose sulphurous odors fill the air
and ashes line the face.

Once Louis, King of France, proclaimed their streams
healthful to fever's cramps
and sent his aching armies to revive
in airs less pungently alive
than their forsaken camp's.

Inside the bay lie our forsaken ships,
as we loud tourists trek,
watching for yellow vipers in the bush—
deadly as spiders—as we push
through underbrush to dock.

Here within the sight of La Pagerie
where Josephine was born,
each Sunday natives rouse themselves at dawn
and take the many paths to town
where churchbells toll them in.

As if in all this gothic machinery,
 weird spires, filagree, and
  stone, you expected to
find a ghost, your eyes search out dark corners
 of the campus, rattling
  like winter winds small bits

of paper. And in these winds, the black-robed
 fathers rush subservi-
  ently on, serving their
apparitions. Into chapel daily,
 they proceed, ever to
  talk of souls like birds im-

prisoned in bone cages of the body.
 Outdoors, in the shadow
  of lost intellects—Joyce,
Lenin, and Voltaire—the lovers' questions
 greet the air with histor-
  ies and inquisitions.

Dimly they sense their minds or souls the caged
 birds of the talk, roofed by
  the robes and spires and stone
and mount dark stairways to the upper floors
 of their minds' silence, think-
  ing to find, locked within,

the mystery of long sweating rooms of stone.
 Instead they find their doubts
  rimed to the wall like frost.
55 Above, freewheeling, birds flock to a clock-

tower, and snow weaves wide,
   white cyclones through the mall.

I come from work, toting my lunchpail
like bouquets of
sweet peas, peonies, or roses,
which you snatch up, oh, so off-handedly!
as if that were the evening's decoration,
the table's frailest centerpiece,
and as if you coquettishly
expected such a gift in return
for simply keeping the whole house in order,
the four walls straight,
the arm chairs neatly turned,
the drapery humming with a harmony of love,
and the evening papers
laid out and neatly folded into news.
And giving it,
I seem to get vast worlds returned
as if inside your throbbing womb
you carried all the childhood woes
of voyaging through Woolworth's all alone.

Out in the Sunday dust our throats go drier,
yelling the red cape from the bull's quick push.
Then we relax, and our blood, taking fire
from crowds about us, crackles like a bush.
For this is Mexico, and living thirsts
in all the wild consuming signs of death.
Here the mere thought of horn and marrow bursts
that silence where a spreading crowd takes breath,
and in hotels across the darkened streets
flesh pours out efforts to remake in one
the two selves cleaving tensely in the sheets
at midnight and the fingerings of dawn.
And wintry Kansas where our trip began
melts in the heat and dust of these concerns,
leaving worn thistles blanching in the sun
of that new lightness which our threshing earns.
Now home, beneath a print that calls the lie
to fear and death, a bull-horn's crushing force
in Manolete's side, we sense his cry,
the spilling wound, and its known anguished course,
and thresh again, anew, those places where
we had our crossings in that morning's heat,
looking for signs of miracles in air
to catch the tinder where two bodies meet.
Ulysses' seven bulls, caught in such fire,
brought back negations he had made to death.
We only catch another, briar to briar,
burning the rooms about us with our breath.

COMMITTAL

"Everything that is not suffered to the end and finally
concluded, recurs, and the same sorrows are undergone."

Hermann Hesse

1

    As your weak runtish son
who feared the fearful bullies of the block
    and wept at almost every sock,
you taught me those dry features of a man
      who bears his pain.

    And imitating that,
I bore your one unchanging look as gain,
    letting no flinch nor sign of strain
betray my endless outward conduit
      of tearless ease.

    Even the bullies found
this ease too toughened to their daily blows.
    Then last month, pain which built its flows
burst, lashing through your ducts the rotting mind
      we had not known.

    Now in the smokeless hue
of psycho-wards we watch your knuckling down
    to take some workless medicine.
Each day we try to stave committing you
      for one more day.

    Like Bernard's famous tank
which you would always use for charity,

our charity becomes a sea
which overflows and will not let us think
or even be.

Your grown sons now, we try
to bear the pains of putting you away.
For your own good, I want to say,
and seem again a runtish, smarting boy
staving his pain.

2

How can we take you home
when here the skirting doctors can't control
the wild ravings and those acts
which forced our making of the pacts
that keep you here blue-shirted and locked-up,
away from harm?

When we were still your boys,
you knowingly eclipsed our wolfish Spark
into that midnight wooden box
and buried him among the phlox
in our backyard, calming us with your look
that played so wise.

Last night you took a chair
to crack against my skull and forced me out.
A senseless act! Even our fence
stands scorched from your new innocence.
When will you learn it's only us you hurt
by all this anger?

Living we've learned to put
things out of mind: from that full broken toy

thrown from our cribs in infancy,
    the girls we mooned on like a puppy,
our boyhood friends, even the thinning threads
    of each new suit.

    Grown like those Spartan men
who ruthlessly would leave a newborn child
    weak and deformed to midnight winds,
      putting it early from their minds,
we shun the ties that daily flood our hearts
    with ceaseless pain.

    And like those lives gone slack,
we must learn now to put you out of mind,
    to box you with the dreams we've lost.
    Our peace of mind is what you've cost.
The doctors say our visits are upsetting.
    We won't be back.

3

    Digging around these graves
for those lost markers of the dead, we damn
    the living for the pure bedlam,
sifting with others the lost, former lives
    that ground this peak.

    As children, mornings you
would take us hiking out across Marsh Creek
    to this overcrowded field, thick
with searchers, and pay death its yearly due
    with vanquished head.

    Now from our separate homes,
we must assume that debtor's role instead,

paying these duties to the dead
who died before we came. A small rain comes,
          and we damn more.

      Still we must search them out,
digging if need be till the fingers sore,
      for goodwill's not sufficient here.
Like death, each ragged plot must be set right
          before we're done.

      Fearing the noon's parade,
the Legion's bright brass band and longer line
      to the slick war memorial's stone,
we try again for markers grasses hide
          and bite our lips.

      Children, we used to wait
impatiently to see these marching troops,
      squared off in separate, tiny groups
of endless seeming, puffed-up, martial dress
          and sparkling plate.

      Fearing we'll be held up,
we blame our having started out so late,
      the florist's sloth, the guarded gate,
each small delay we think of as we grope
          from stone to way.

      Finding, thinking we'd found
all of the plots, we're out of words to say.
      My God, how is it sons allay
these restless ghosts they've only known as ground?
          We stand spent stone.

      Father, they were your hope
as we, too willful, have become our own.

Driven insane, you march alone
in wards to teach us pains our lives envelop.
We learn and go.

4

Forcing ourselves to work,
to note again the senseless bric-a-brac,
we pass the day into a week
while life goes playing hide-and-seek
and won't disturb the slow meanderings
nor bring us back.

Among the furniture
you hide and I inside my bookish chair
until your dusting brings two clowns
off from their windowed perch and downs
them headless on the noisy frontroom floor
and shows us here.

The boys come running down
to chide us harshly for our murderous din.
I quell them, telling them to wait;
in time the clowns will be set straight,
and find myself awakening to the shock
as if to pain,

and think of promises
my father made to quell our noisy shouts,
hanging about his bullish neck
like some unconquerable peak,
that one by one he failed to see quite through
or else forgot:

the car he promised,
the b.b. gun, or trips we never took,

dreams sidelined for another day
that coming turned our heads away
until his promises were playschool stores
devoid of stock.

Now in his psycho-ward
struggling against his daily medicines,
he lives, and I know I must live,
giving what comfort I can give,
filling this hope unable to fill his.
Thus childhood ends.

They run back to their games,
asking where I'd been staying and so long.
Happy the clowns will be like new,
sons disappear into a blue,
leaving their words to seek their fathers out.
Where? Where've you gone?